Super Prestige

Sheffield

Philip Battersby

D1335439

© 2002 Venture Publications Ltd

ISBN 1 898432 82 1

Front cover: A Sheffield AEC Regent hard at work - No. **116** (**OWE 116**) at Sharrow Head in 1962, and since preserved.

Inside front: Further AEC Regents, each approximately ten years old when photographed, were Nos **117** (**OWE 117**) and **1369** (**369 HWE**). In the upper view outside the Midland railway station in 1963, the accompanying red vehicle is an East Midland Leyland Atlantean. In the lower view in 1973, the successor is a Leyland National in East Midland's NBC green.

Rear cover: Sheffield possessed one of the greatest British tramway systems, typified latterly by Standard car **164** of 1933 and Roberts car **523** of 1951, seen *(upper)* at Market Side in 1957. The origins of the system are represented by horse-tram **15** of 1874, seen *(lower)* on active display at the National Tramway Museum, Crich, in 1991. *(John A Senior; John Banks)*

Inside rear: Leyland driver-training bus No. **M2** (**KWA 552**) *(upper)* was freshly turned out in the reversed livery upon transfer from the passenger fleet in 1962. It had previously been No. 552. At the same time, AEC Regent No. **324** (**KWB 924**) *(lower)* with distinctive Roberts coachwork was still in normal use. *(Cover pictures by John Lythgoe except where stated.)*

Title page: Car **65,** built in Queens Road works, was a 1930 example of Sheffield's new Standard tram and was photographed on a 10ins x 8ins glass plate negative. *(Richard Moore archive)*

Below: Passengers galore! The peak period of passenger demand in the postwar years is graphically illustrated by this view of 1947 AEC Regent No. **582** (**KWB 82**) at Pond Street bus station. *(G H F Atkins)*

Opposite page: The Eastern Coach Works body was the subject of this magnificent study featuring Leyland PD2/20 No. **1293** (**YWB 293**) at the Dore terminus of route 50 in August 1962. *(John Lythgoe)*

Page 4: Number **150** was the last survivor of 25 trams built for Sheffield by W. Hill & Co., of South Shields. This view in Stubbin Lane shows the car city-bound from Sheffield Lane Top on the last day of the route, 2nd April 1960. *(John Lythgoe)*

Introduction and Acknowledgements

The city of Sheffield, with a population in excess of a half-million, has a proud record in the annals of passenger transport. This has been achieved by the outstanding quality of Sheffield Transport Department, by the South Yorkshire Passenger Transport Authority with its far-reaching low fares policy, and now by Supertram. It is therefore not surprising that many publications on Sheffield's transport have appeared across the years. Among them I have found the following to be of particular help:-

Modern Tramway magazine, issues 240/2/3, articles by R J S Wiseman (Light Railway Transport League, 1957-58)
The Sheffield Joint Omnibus Committee by C T Humpidge (The Omnibus Society, 1963)
Sheffield Transport by Charles C Hall (Transport Publishing Company, 1977)
Sheffield Corporation Tramways by Kenneth Gandy (Sheffield City Libraries, 1985)
Sheffield Trams Remembered by Graham Hague and Howard Turner (Sheaf Publishing, 1987)
A Nostalgic Look at Sheffield Trams Since 1950 by Graham H E Twidale (Silver Link, 1995)
Lost Sheffield by Peter Machan (ALD Design & Print, 2000)

This book divides into two main parts, and in the first I describe the Richard Moore archive on which that part is based. The photographs in it are taken from his archive unless otherwise acknowledged, and I am particularly grateful to his daughter Mrs Brenda Barker for so kindly making them available. A similar generous and much-valued offer of material has resulted in the second part of the book being built around the photography of John R H Lythgoe, and in the same manner the pictures there were taken by John unless individually credited. Other pictures are from the Senior Transport Archive *(STA)*: some STA prints were issued with free reproduction rights by Leyland Motors and where the negatives are known to have passed to the British Commercial Vehicle Museum *(BCVM)*, the museum's courtesy in allowing their use is appreciated; Geoffrey Atkins has provided many views from his legendary collection; other pictures are from my own camera. The immense meticulous efforts of John Lythgoe, Geoff Allen, Charles Hall, Tom Robinson and Ron Maybray have provided detailed factual information, and The PSV Circle has permitted the use of its many publications. Ian Currie, Geoff Allen and Paul Fox have helped with corrections, and Series Editor John Banks has given unstinting assistance and guidance. I thank them all.

This book is not a comprehensive history of Sheffield Transport Department, nor is it an information handbook. It is a graphic survey that will enable you to travel through the years of the undertaking's growth and success, but as with any transport tour, you cannot go everywhere and see everything. You will see things you didn't know about, and revisit scenes you thought you had forgotten, but I apologise for any mistakes which might have crept in, and for anything which you would like to have seen but which has not managed to find a space between these covers.

Philip Battersby
Middlesbrough, April 2002

4

The City of Sheffield

Before we start looking at the pictures, it is worth looking at a few of the milestones in the development of the city. This development both created a need for town transport and was made possible by it. The town's population was 45,000 in 1801. During the reign of Queen Victoria (1837-1901) it grew from 100,000 to 400,000. The borough was incorporated in 1843 and city status was achieved fifty years later in 1893. The Sheffield University was opened in 1905, and the Diocese of Sheffield was created in 1913, whereupon the ancient parish church was designated its cathedral.

The Sheffield Joint Omnibus Committee

The main line railway companies had obtained parliamentary powers in 1928 to operate motor buses, a step designed to protect their interests against this rapidly developing competitor. Although they began by operating buses in their own names, the railways soon changed to an indirect approach. Many successful independent local businesses were competing against large companies, and welcomed the railways' offer of capital investment. This usually took the form of establishing a limited company involving the existing proprietors but controlled by the railway company. On a much bigger scale, the railways then bought into the main territorial companies, and rationalised their position by transferring to them their shares in the smaller companies. The whole process greatly increased the size of the big territorial companies, and gave them a strong presence even in cities with flourishing municipal operators. Instances such as Ribble and Crosville in Liverpool or Hants & Dorset in Southampton readily come to mind.

Sheffield did not really have a territorial bus company. Rather, it was the meeting place of several such as East Midland, Yorkshire Traction and even North Western, coming into the city from different directions. Neither was Sheffield wholly in the territory of any one railway company, and when it came to dealing with bus services in the area, the London &

North Eastern and the London, Midland & Scottish Railways acted jointly and approached Sheffield Corporation. The result was the creation of the Sheffield Joint Omnibus Committee, with three categories of operation. Services entirely within the 1929 Sheffield city boundary were the sole property of the Corporation and constituted category A. Long distance services to places such as Manchester, Gainsborough and Bradford belonged entirely to the railway companies and were identified as category C. In between the two was category B, medium-distance services crossing the city boundary and operated jointly by the railways and the Corporation with an agreed sharing of expenses and receipts.

In day to day operation, the vehicles and services in all three categories were operated by the Corporation, who acted as agents for the railways in all respects. To the observer, all the buses were in the Sheffield colours of cream and blue, and in post-war years all carried the "Sheffield" fleetname. Their actual ownership was indicated on the vehicles by the letters A, B or C, and the legal lettering varied accordingly although the address "Division Street, Sheffield" was the same for them all. Prior to the 1948 nationalisation of the railways, the LNER and LMS had a further agreement between themselves. Under this they individually held the separate assets which when taken together constituted the railway holdings on the Joint Committee.

Not only was the Joint Committee itself quite a complex scheme, but many of its services were jointly operated. Over the years this involved three other municipalities and five major companies.

Under the terms of the Transport Act of 1968 the railway assets passed to the National Bus Company. In the consequent reorganization some of the services of the Joint Committee went to the Corporation at the end of 1969, and others to subsidiaries of the NBC. In this way, the Sheffield Joint Omnibus Committee came to an end after over forty years of successful working.

LONDON & NORTH EASTERN RAILWAY COMPANY.
R.C. MOORE. M. INST. T.
DIVISION STREET.
SHEFFIELD

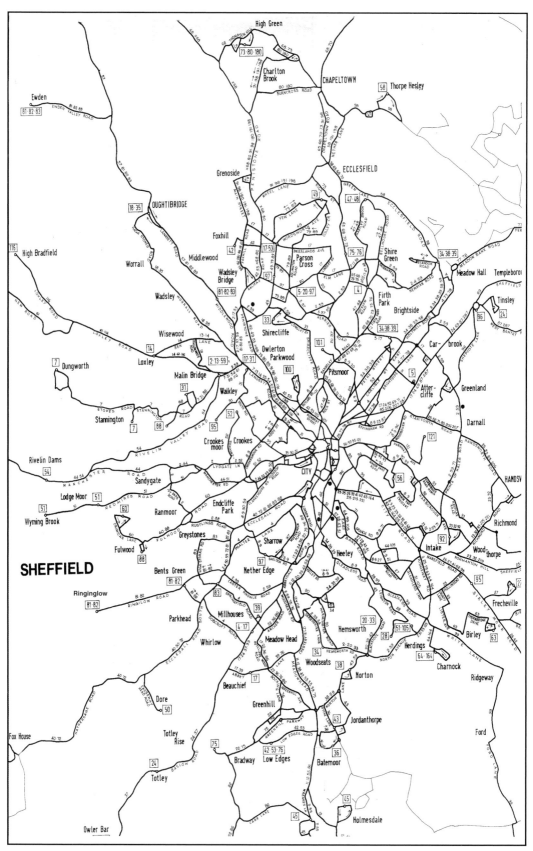

SHEFFIELD

Above: The final year of the undertaking, 1973, is typified by new Leyland Atlantean No. **317** (**UWA 317L**) with East Lancashire bodywork. *(G H F Atkins)*

Sheffield City Transport   1973

ROTHERHAM

Dalton

Sitwell Park

Canklow

BRINSWORTH

Treeton

Orgreave

AUGHTON

Woodhouse Mill

Aston

Woodhouse

DINNINGTON

Todwick Bar

North Anston

Todwick

South Anston

Hackenthorpe

BEIGHTON

Waleswood

Kiveton Park

Sothall

Wales Bar

Wales

Halfway

Norwood

MOSBOROUGH

ECKINGTON

- S.C.T. depôts
- S.C.T. bus routes and termini
- Other bus routes

SCALES   Miles   © Ashton Gray 1977

Kilometres

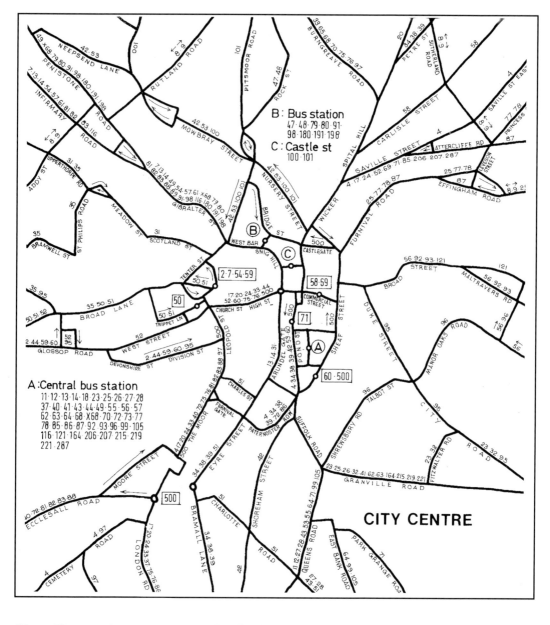

Maps: The map shown across pages 6 and 7 depicts the Sheffield City Transport bus network in 1973, and includes the routes previously operated by the Sheffield Joint Omnibus Committee. It shows the maximum extent of operations prior to the absorption of the undertaking into the South Yorkshire Passenger Transport Authority in 1974. The city centre inset is presented separately above. The growth of the city and the ever greater complexity of the bus route network means that only a few years after the abandonment of the tramways their former routes were not readily apparent from the bus map. Nevertheless the names of the tram termini mentioned in the text mostly appear here, although more as district names than as precise terminal points. However, it might be useful to note that 'Ecclesall' could be added just right of Bents Green, 'Sheffield Lane Top' to the left of Shiregreen, and 'Elm Tree' left of Intake. The letters A, B and C on the city centre map identify the locations of three separate bus terminals and do not refer to the three Sheffield fleets mentioned in the text. The Central bus station is frequently described as Pond Street and is opposite the Midland railway station. The others are Bridge Street bus station and Castle Street respectively. The maps were prepared by Ashton Gray for the Transport Publishing Company in 1977 and first appeared in the book *Sheffield Transport* in that year.

PART ONE

The Richard Moore Archive

The Tramway Era in Sheffield is a 32-page booklet which takes its place with pride amongst a distinctive type of publication, the Souvenir Brochure. It was issued by Sheffield Transport Department on the closure of the tramways on 8th October 1960. Over the years, similar brochures have been issued not only for tramway closures but for jubilees and centenaries, and not only by municipal transport departments but also by company undertakings. The Sheffield example stood out for two reasons. First, it was about the trams, and resisted the temptation to be a showcase for the City Council or the Transport Committee. In this booklet you did not find pictures or lists of civic worthies, nor even a list of General Managers or other officials of the Transport Department. Second, although the trams were being replaced by buses, and the reasons were explained, the book was undoubtedly a celebration of the tramcar and in no sense a celebration of the motor bus. Events had clearly invoked a feeling of regret about the inevitability of the whole business, and if we had to say good-bye to the trams, it was to be done in the most appreciative manner possible. Nevertheless the task of compiling and producing this Souvenir Brochure was done with great professionalism, demonstrated by the restrained, balanced and objective text which briefly presented the history of the city's tramways.

One of the men behind the scenes whose faithful service created both the tramways and the Souvenir Brochure was Richard L Moore, doubly anonymous because the mention of his name will cause the reader to think that he was the R C Moore whose name appeared on the sides of the Transport Department's trams and buses from 1945 to 1961. He was not, although we can add here that Rowland Claude Moore was also a native of Sheffield, and had commenced his career with the Department in 1914. Between 1929 and 1943 he held posts at Stockton, Hull and Liverpool before returning to Sheffield.

Richard Lawson Moore, four or five years younger, was born in 1900 and spent his whole working life with the Sheffield Transport Department. In his early days as an office junior he was known as 'Rattles'

because one of his tasks was to travel on vehicles to listen for any untoward rattles and report them for attention. Latterly he was Chief Traffic Assistant or, more formally, Assistant Traffic Superintendent (Operations), with responsibility for platform staff, the bus stations and all highway matters. This involved numerous meetings with police and highway authorities about the details of tram and bus operation. Outside work, he was an active member of the Methodist church and a local preacher. He also had a great interest in walking in the countryside and regularly contributed rambling features to the local newspaper. He was a man of character, with sterling qualities.

Most notably, Richard had a particular interest and skill in photography, to the extent that it became part of his work with the Department, recording vehicles, accidents and historic events. The official Last Tram archival ciné film was made by him. He continued with the undertaking until his retirement in 1966, and subsequently retained a wide range of photographs, glass negatives and lantern slides which in the modernisation mania of the 1960s would otherwise surely have ended up in the bin. That collection is the starting point for this book.

Richard had made use of much of the material in compiling the 1960 Souvenir Brochure, and its renewed availability gives us the opportunity to see it again. It is, after all, more than forty years since that brochure, published as a numbered special edition and available only through the Transport

Department, made its appearance. It was never intended to be more than it said, a Souvenir. The comprehensive history *Sheffield Transport* followed later from our predecessor the Transport Publishing Company, and it too was the work of a man who had spent a lifetime with Sheffield Transport Department, Charles C Hall. Even this monumental work has now been in existence for a quarter of a century, and Kenneth Gandy's splendid *Sheffield Corporation Tramways*, published by the Sheffield City Libraries, has been with us seventeen years.

Two other reasons urge us to present some of Richard Moore's work again. The first is the previously unimaginable progress that has been made in the technology of publishing in recent years. It is now possible to present the pictures enlarged and enhanced well beyond anything that could have been achieved in 1960. The second is the handicap which the original producers inadvertently placed upon themselves in the form of colour. Modern colour printing could not have been dreamed of, but in 1960 producers and packagers were on the threshold of an explosion of colour which was seen as a reaction to years of austerity and shortages. The use of a variety of inks to create blocks of colour across a page, thereby highlighting margins, captions, tables and photographs was a bold venture at the time, but when a black and white photograph was presented as black and pink or black and yellow, it was a victory of image over quality. The printers of *The Tramway Era in Sheffield* had used this technique, but like most things where image takes precedence, the product would have been better without it. This was indeed a fashion of the times. Similar booklets produced in the same period by the Potteries and the South Wales bus companies had the same feature, and Sunderland did it as late as 1973. The opportunity to see the pictures from Richard Moore's collection without the superimposed colour is one worth having.

Nevertheless, this book is by no means a re-presentation of the Souvenir Brochure, nor is it a book only or primarily about the trams. True, the Sheffield tramway system was not only eminently successful but was also one of the largest in Britain. Even so, when the Transport Department reached its zenith in 1950 with 1002 vehicles, 559 of them were motor buses, and Richard Moore's collection of official and other photographs recorded their progress too.

Part of the huge development which led to the Department's motor buses outnumbering its tramcars was the expansion of housing. The clearance of closely packed slum housing in favour of the 'garden cities' of the 1930s and the 'estates' of the 1940s and 1950s created large new areas requiring transport, particularly to and from the city centre. Although we could not reasonably have expected the designers to foresee today's widespread car ownership, we can be surprised that some new estates not only failed to have a 'backbone' route suitable for an intensive service of either trams or buses, but consisted only of narrow roads little suited to any sort of transport provision. Nevertheless, transport was provided, initially by strategic but short tramway extensions. Significantly longer extensions were subsequently made by new bus services which often overlapped the tram routes. Over a long period, the trams gradually lost a lot of passengers, not only by the demolition of old houses, but also by having to share their clientele with ever more buses operating alongside. The 1951 decision to replace the tramways in their entirety held sway for forty years before fresh thinking led to the emergence of the 'supertrams' of the present day.

This pattern of motor bus expansion in Sheffield was no more than was to be found in towns and cities elsewhere, and the bigger the city, the more pronounced was the growth. However there was another factor, strongly characteristic of Sheffield, which made a highly significant contribution to the size of the bus fleet. This was the creation, with effect from 1st January 1929, of the Sheffield Joint Omnibus Committee, as already described. At its formation the Joint Committee accounted for 69 buses wholly or partially owned by the railway companies against only 57 owned outright by the Corporation. This was of course when the city's tram fleet vastly outnumbered the buses. By 1963, after all the trams had gone, the Corporation's own fleet was far larger than the Joint Committee's. Nevertheless the latter accounted for 221 vehicles.

The glory days have now passed, but this book aims to bring them again to the forefront of our minds, and who better than Richard Moore to be our guide as we turn the pages and look through the archive he so carefully and lovingly collected?

Lost Sheffield

Above: Horse-drawn buses in Sheffield had beginnings as early as 1834. With notable expansion from about 1852, a considerable network of services under several proprietors was operating by 1873. This picture shows Castle Street, itself eventually to become a motor-bus terminus, at the crossing with Waingate, from which early tram services, also horse-drawn, departed for Attercliffe and Brightside. The Royal Hotel, demolished in 1914, is here facing the photographer from the crossroads corner. *Below:* Much of the Victorian city centre consisted of narrow streets, with both buses and trams operating from the edge of this congested area out to the suburbs. In this view looking down High Street we can note Foster's outfitters shop, the firm which held out longest for compensation prior to the dramatic road widening of 1896. High Street subsequently became a major bus and tram artery in a network of cross-city services, and achieved national notoriety a century later during the bus wars which saw it blocked solid.

Horse Buses

Above: Proprietor William Henry Haigh did not intend his premises on the corner of Cemetery Road and Ecclesall Road to pass unnoticed. He had commenced about 1862, and became the city's major horse-bus operator from 1872-73 after the demise of the Sheffield Carriage Company and the retirement of competitor Charles Thompson. He retained this status until he withdrew from bus operation in 1890. *Below:* Various operators in turn ran on the hilly Springvale route over the years from 1862. This rear view some thirty years later is an excellent study of the 'knifeboard' upper-deck seat arrangement with double staircase. The conductor is about to climb the wrong one to collect the fares of two ladies and a gentleman. The view down Fargate towards High Street is largely blocked by the end of Foster's shop shown on the previous page. By the time of this picture the operator was the Springvale and Upperthorpe company of 1883, and the route had been extended to Walkley over gradients of even greater severity.

Horse Buses

Above: After the withdrawal of W H Haigh from the scene in 1890, one of the two most significant bus operators was Reuben Thompson whose services had developed in the previous decade. His Ecclesall Road bus was seen at Hunter's Bar very smartly presented, and he had a reputation for high standards of luxury and service. Despite the extension of tramway routes from 1896 and their electrification from 1899, Thompson continued to operate until at least 1900. *Below:* The other notable operator of the 1890s was Joseph Tomlinson, who had commenced operations by 1875. His more modern bus with garden-seat upper deck was the final type of horse-bus, and is seen operating to Pitsmoor and Osgathorpe in the north of the city.

Horse Trams

The Sheffield Tramways Company commenced operation in 1873 under a lease from the Corporation, who built and owned the track. The five routes were completed by 1877, and worked initially by 45 cars. Each route had its own depot and cars, and there was no physical connection between the two southern and the three northern routes. On this page are shown two of the 1877 eight-window single-deckers on the Nether Edge route. Above, the two horses bring No. **45** up the hill in Montgomery Road, and below No. **44** waits at the outer terminus .

Horse Trams

Above: Double-deck car **9** of 1873 survived to be acquired by the Corporation upon expiry of the Company's operating lease. The car body was rather bowed by the time of this late picture in Tinsley depot yard, and the solemnity of the occasion, with Mr Mallyon the top-hatted manager, might indicate a photograph taken to mark the transfer in July 1896. Nowadays the building is home to the Sheffield Bus Museum. *Below:* The Corporation lost little time in deciding to extend and electrify the system. This scene at the bottom of The Moor in 1898 shows new track for Ecclesall Road going off to the left, and replacement tracks for the Nether Edge and Heeley routes (centre and right). They were all operated by horse traction pending electrification, but the Ellin Street line (middle backround, right) was never completed or used.

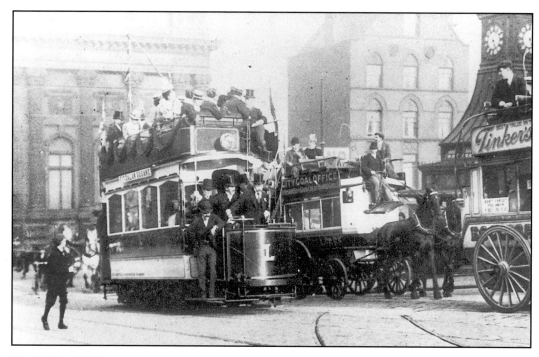

Early Electric Trams

Above: On 5th September 1899 the electric tramways were formally opened, and the official party, driven by the Lord Mayor, was photographed on car No. **1** at Fitzalan Square. The passengers and drivers on Reuben Thompson's horse buses would have recognised the event as the beginning of the end for their form of conveyance. *Below:* The magnificent buildings of the recently widened High Street formed an imposing background for this view of cars **2** and **11** on the first full day of electric operation, 6th September. Nevertheless it took until November 1901 to sort out track and traffic problems and establish a system of cross-city services.

Early Electric Trams

Above: Before the end of the same month, September 1899, service had commenced on the Walkley and Pitsmoor routes. Single-deck cars were used because these routes were steeply graded, and this 1900 view shows new Brush car No. **94** at Pitsmoor. *Below:* By the end of 1904 the electric passenger fleet totalled 241, an indication of the phenomenal growth of the system in just over five years. Of these, 168 had been delivered as short-canopy open-top double-deckers like Brush-built No. **239** shown here in 1905. The Chantrey Arms at Norton Woodseats in Chesterfield Road had been reached in April 1903, and remained the terminus until the short extension to Abbey Lane corner in 1923.

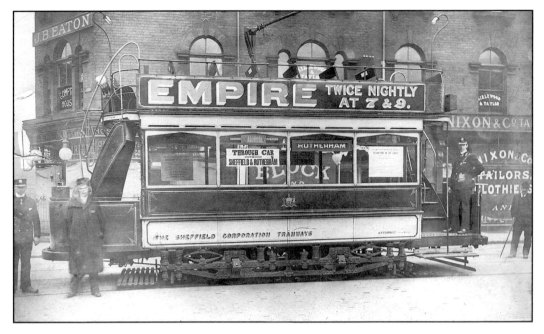

Edwardian Trams

Above: From the neighbouring town of Rotherham the trams had reached Tinsley in July 1903. Connection of the two systems at this point enabled a joint through service between Sheffield and Rotherham centres to commence in September 1905. The occasion was marked by this photograph of an unidentified Sheffield car in College Square, Rotherham. The picture incidentally affords a good view of the Peckham Cantilever truck. *Below:* An extensive programme of fitting top covers to double deckers commenced in 1903, with an immediate increase in revenue. The design reflected fears that extended canopies would put too much strain on the body structure. Car **246** was the first in the fleet to be so fitted from new, and was built in the Corporation's own workshops at Nether Edge. The winter scene would mark its entry into service in January 1905. Note the "tram station" legend on the street lamp.

Edwardian Trams

Above: The city's East End was significantly opened up by the electric trams, illustrated here by car **37** at The Wicker bound for Handsworth. The destination "Sheffield" on car **87** approaching the camera indicates a journey into town on the joint service from Rotherham, circa 1910-11. Both cars were withdrawn in 1922, but 37 went to Gateshead where it ran until 1950-51. *Below:* Number **250** was another of the first (1905) batch of cars to be top-covered from new. However, this picture at Millhouses a few years later clearly shows a 21E-type truck, in marked contrast to the Milnes girder truck under car 246 opposite.

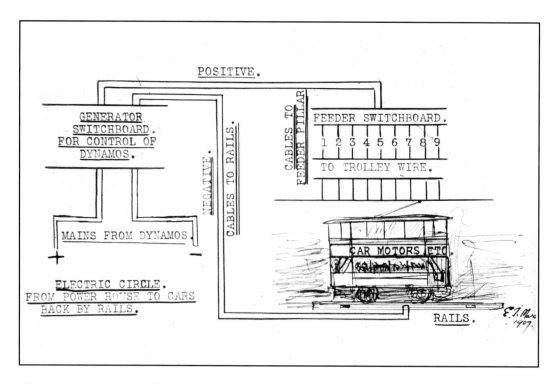

Giving an Illustrated Talk - 1

A lantern slide lecture in the days before cinema, radio and television was a rare treat for schools, church groups and institutes. The Tramways Department performed a significant educational role with such lectures, and would create a sound foundation by beginning with basic principles. Here are *(above)* the main electric circuit, drawn in 1907, and *(below)* the arrangement of the connections inside the controller.

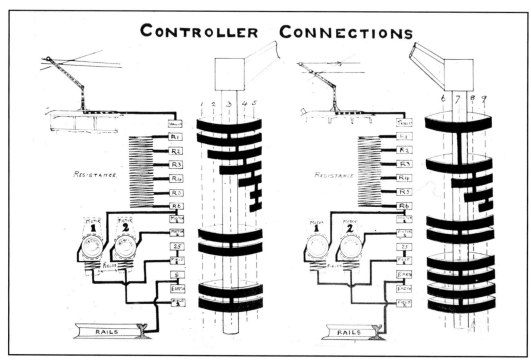

Giving an Illustrated Talk - 2

Above: "Seeing how it works" followed the theory, with the removal of the floor hatches affording a view of the motors. The cover has been removed to show how to reach the brushes for maintenance, but the gear casings remain in place. More noteworthy 95 years later are the short-lived seat cushions redolent of the horse-bus era. *Below:* A view of the truck when detached from the body underframe, with the opportunity taken to remove the gear casings and see the toothed gear wheels which transmitted the drive. This 21E-type truck contrasts with its Peckham Cantilever equivalent under the car in the background.

More Edwardian Trams

Above: The large number of cars with short top covers created a 'Sheffield look', although many other systems had similar designs, including London United, Huddersfield and Preston. In this slightly later picture dating from about 1913, car **59** in Fitzalan Square was being followed by single-decker **53** bound for Walkley, and the motor-car **O 4570** of 1910-11 was a sign of things to come.
Below: When Aubrey Llewellyn Coventry Fell left Sheffield at the end of 1903 to make his name with the London County Council Tramways, his successor as General Manager was Arthur Robinson Fearnley. The new man introduced the extended canopy style to the fleet with this rebuild of single-deck car **208**, completed in 1906.

A New Reign

Above: The end of the Edwardian era is vividly illustrated by this view of car **162** decorated for the coronation of King George V in June 1911. The car itself is another 1906-07 single-deck rebuild with longer platforms, full-length top deck and canopy. With their five-bay bodies, these cars typically seated 68 or 72, whereas new vestibuled four-bay cars of otherwise similar design seated 58, and the short-ended cars usually only 51.

Right: Another 1911 addition to the fleet was the first motorised tower wagon. The locally-built Durham-Churchill chassis was registered **W 1428**.

Despite the appearance of the full-length canopy on twenty-seven cars in 1906-07, the short top-cover continued to be used for the enclosing of open cars until 1910. Thereafter the style shown here on car **11** was adopted, this one being rebuilt from open-top in 1913. The programme to cover all the open-toppers was completed in that year.

Early Motor Buses - 1

Above: From February 1913 passengers for Lodge Moor hospital could alight from the Fulwood tram at Broomhill and board the Department's new motor-bus which ran via Manchester Road. Number **9 (W 3880)** was a 36-seat Daimler CC with Dodson body which joined the infant fleet in September of that year. This view shows the bus in Leadmill Road outside Shoreham Street tram depot where the buses were initially housed. *Below:* Some 18 AEC Y-type variants were purchased in 1920-21 with both single- and double-deck bodies, and all but one survived until at least 1926. The original of this picture is inscribed by Richard Moore in impeccable handwriting, "Market Place, Chapeltown in 1926. The West Riding County Council propose to construct a traffic island at this road junction." Perhaps those proposals came many years after the picture, because apart from the AEC bus, the traffic which would have circumnavigated the proposed island is notably absent.

Giving an Illustrated Talk - 3

The declaration of war in August 1914 was the start of a very difficult period. The Department recruited conductresses from June 1915, and eight young ladies are seen *(above)* in the training school. The tutor is explaining timetables, duty sheets and running boards. Later, he would teach them how to release the handbrake from the back platform, and how to apply it in an emergency. The 41 conductresses lined up for an official photograph *(below)* were probably the first batch to be passed out, hence the sense of occasion. The ladies were to number 680 at the peak of their involvement before the men returned in 1919.

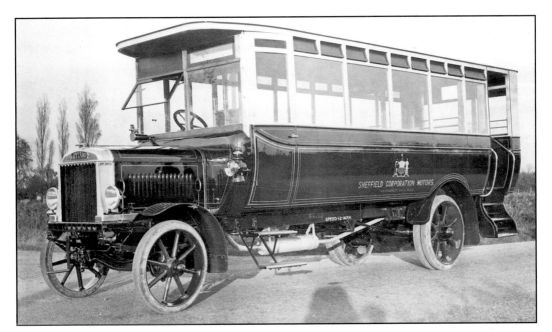

Early Motor Buses - 2

Above: This manufacturer's photograph of an M-type for Sheffield was recorded by Leyland's clerk on 14th October 1921. This virtually proves the vehicle, which cannot be identified from the picture itself, to have been No. **16** (**WA 5325**) which entered service on 28th of the same month. *Below:* Number **56** (**WB 503**) of July 1924 was the Department's first top-covered double-deck bus, although the whole tram fleet had already been so configured for the previous eleven years. The Brush 52-seat body on the AEC 504 chassis was remarkably commodious for the period, and an immediate success. The short spur tram route to Petre Street was replaced by similar buses in 1925.

Pneumatic Tyres

Above: The undertaking's first bus to be fitted with pneumatic tyres was Leyland No. **49 (WA 9601)**, which entered service in March 1924. The taking of the photograph at a bleak moorland location was probably combined with a test run.

Below: The development of the 'side type' of chassis, with the driver alongside the engine instead of behind it in the arrangement later usually called 'forward control', was another notable feature. Five such machines on the AEC 503-type chassis arrived early in 1925. This one, by then in the B fleet, was No. **68 (WB 2139)**, seen at work in Pond Street in September 1929. The AEC 503 and 504 chassis were still straight-framed, and were minor variants of the London General Omnibus Company's successful S class. *(G H F Atkins)*

Three-axle Double-deckers

Above: Guy buses made an appearance in the fleet in 1925, with repeat orders, all being single-deckers. A spectacular three-axle double-decker came in 1927, an FCX with Guy 60-seat body. In a setting with the air of a stately home, this view of No. **131** (**WE 40**) shows the double step on to the platform which indicates a straight-framed chassis. *Below:* Number **133** (**WE 1467**) of 1928 was the second of two Karrier WL6 three-axle double-deckers. By the time of this photograph, the vehicle had joined the B fleet, and its 60-seat Karrier body was lettered to show the railway involvement.

Above: A neater vehicle was the Leyland-bodied ineptly-named Titanic No. **136** (**WE4381**); Leyland's filing clerk dated this picture as 1st July 1929. Note the extra front doorway, and the low platform made possible by a dropped-frame chassis. *(STA/BCVM)*

Single-deck Progress

Leyland TS1 Tiger No. **141** (**WE 3061**) entered service in December 1928, with body design combining a rakish front with a back end looking distinctly chopped off. The service-number box was a typical Sheffield addition. This is a September 1934 Pond Street scene. *(G H F Atkins)*

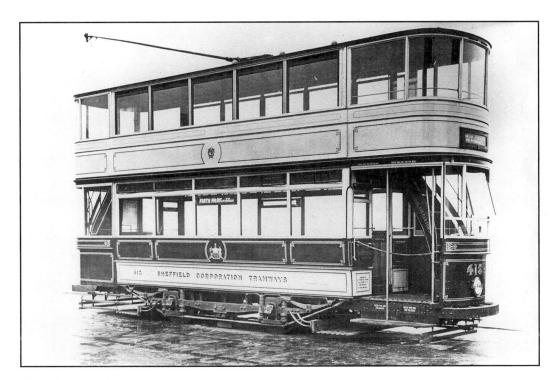

New Trams by the Hundred

Although the motor-bus fleet had expanded energetically in the 14 years since its inception in 1913, in the same period the already large tram fleet was augmented and improved by well over 200 new cars. Seventy-five balcony cars in 1912-15 were followed by 154 enclosed cars in 1918-27. The latter were large cars which significantly increased the fleet's total carrying capacity, but the 76 seats in No. **413** *(above)* must have been a tight squeeze. The 2-and-1 upper saloon seating in the final batch, as in No. **460** *(below)*, reduced the total to 68.

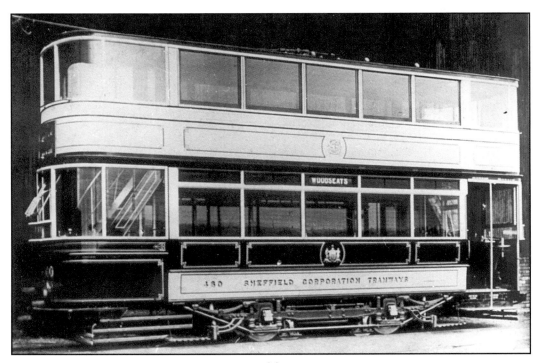

New Trams by the Hundred

Many of the balcony cars were later enclosed, and had a typical life span of 20 to 24 years. The enclosed cars like Nos **386** and **449** shown here were subsequently fitted with air brakes and ran for 30 to 35 or more years. They retained their "rocker panel" design in which the side walls curved inwards to bring the weight directly on to the main underframe. By the 1950s this looked distinctly old-fashioned. Car 386 *(above)* was photographed in Angel Street, and car 449 at Midland Station, both in the city centre. *(G H F Atkins)*

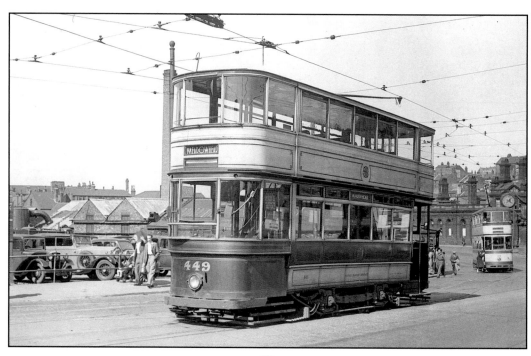

Giving an Illustrated Talk - 4

A lantern slide show could sometimes involve showing an audience things that were there to be seen all the time! An example is this view *(above)* of the overhead power feeder point. On the other hand, scenes like the one below, of the ticket office in the Division Street headquarters, were most definitely 'behind the scenes'.

Early Leyland Titans

Above: The revolutionary Leyland TD1 Titan combined a dropped-frame chassis with the patented sunken side gangway in the upper saloon to produce a double-decker of unprecedented low height. Number **1** (**WE 4371**) of 1929 is seen behind the GPO in the northern part of Pond Street. *(G H F Atkins)*

Below: Over the years, care was generally taken to match the fleet and registration numbers, but the practice was only in its infancy when TD1 No. **33** entered service in August 1928 registered **WE 2932**. The photograph was taken later in the same year on the Inner Circle route. *(STA/BCVM)*

More New Trams

Above: A tram which became a new standard for the future was No. **1** of 1927. With what had become the new 'Sheffield look' of the 1920s, the car had a straight-sided modern appearance, and upholstered 2-and-1 seating in both saloons. The cost of comfort was a reduction in capacity to 61. In this postwar scene, the car loads at Market Side for Tinsley (Weedon Street). *(G H F Atkins)*

Right: Number **370** of 1931 looked the same but was different. Known as the Duralumin tram because of its aluminium frame, it ran for 26 years but remained unique. Here it was pushing the trolley as it left Tenter Street depot.

Tiger Development

Above: The Leyland Tiger with Leyland body had developed apace since the 1928 model shown on page 30. Number **124 (WE 9824)** of 1930 was a TS1 with sloping canopy, and a folding door at the extreme rear. It was in the A fleet and carried the city's title and coat of arms.

Below: Number **216 (WJ 3556)** of 1932 with level canopy presented a more attractive modern appearance, but the doorway, now of the porch style, had been moved forward and was flanked by two small windows giving a more cluttered look to the body side. This TS4 model was in the C fleet, lettered "L.M.S. and L.N.E. Railways", and was sold after only six years of service. *(Both: STA/BCVM)*

Titans Under Observation

Above: Brand new Leyland TD1 No. **173** (**WE 8773**) was caught by Leyland's photographer ascending the 1 in 11 gradient in Glossop Road in July 1930. The Crosspool service traversed Glossop and Manchester Roads which were not served by trams. *Below:* A much tougher proposition was the 1 in 6 of Crookesmoor Road in the same locality, being tackled by No. **161** (**WE 7061**) delivered a few months earlier. The Circular service was introduced in July 1929, and became the 'Inner Circle' two years later when the 'Outer Circle' commenced. *(Both: STA/BCVM)*

Titans Under Observation

The two views on this page are also on Crookesmoor Road in July 1930, and no doubt Leyland's photographers were simply accompanying their engineers. In successive pictures the bus is No. **169** (**WE 8769**), new in June. The lower view shows that this vehicle did not have a rear emergency exit, whereas the buses on the previous page had two. This topic, and that of the dimensions of the back platform cut-away, was a cause for some concern to the Ministry of Transport at the time when extensive new legislation was being framed. *(Both: STA/BCVM)*

London and North Eastern Railway

Above: The Sheffield style of destination box gave some semblance of similarity to a quite different body design from Leyland's own, in this case by the railway wagon builder Charles Roberts of Horbury near Wakefield. Number **225** (**WJ 7725**) in the C fleet was a petrol-engined Tiger TS6 of 1933. *Below:* The same body was specified for AEC Regal No. **198** (**AWA998**) in 1934. Both these vehicles were owned outright by the LNER and were painted in its apple green livery at first. Their lettering reads "James McLaren, Secretary, Marylebone Station, London N.W.1", but they were numbered in Sheffield's fleet. *(Both: G H F Atkins)*

Railway Buses in Sheffield Livery

Above: Another Roberts-bodied Leyland Tiger was No. **12 (WJ 7212)** on the TS4 chassis, supplied for the B fleet in 1933. In this case the Sheffield dark blue and cream livery was carried, with a composite Sheffield, LMS and LNER fleetname. Individual ownership by Sheffield Corporation was shown in the legal lettering.

Below: Distinctive local Cravens bodywork was fitted to No. **214 (WJ 7214)**, another Leyland TS4 of 1933, but this time for the C fleet. Although the Sheffield livery was carried, only the railway companies appeared in the fleetname, and the legal lettering showed this vehicle to be individually owned by the LNER, albeit under the General Manager at Sheffield Corporation's Division Street headquarters. *(Both: STA)*

Further Leyland Titanics

Above: Although numerous repeat orders were placed for the Leyland Titan, the three-axle double-decker was not immediately eclipsed. Number **108 (WJ 4608)** was one of five TT2 Titanics received in 1932. The Leyland bodies seated only 28 on each deck, which in the case of the lower saloon was partly because of the front doorway shown here. *Below:* The low seating capacity upstairs was explained by the alternate rows of three and four seats. *(Both: STA/BCVM)*

Standard Trams

Above: After the introduction of new tram No. 1 in 1927, the type went into production in 1928 and replaced many older cars. In this postwar scene, No. **198** was loading at the top of Angel Street for a journey to Fulwood, which in 1952 was the first route to go in the eventual general abandonment programme. *(G H F Atkins) Below:* The new Standards had reached the colossal total of 210 cars when production ceased in 1936. Car **224** was a 1935 example, and illustrates the new cream livery with a lighter shade of blue introduced with car 203 in that year.

Standard Trams

Above: The Standard car in the new livery is well illustrated by this view of No. **218** freshly completed in 1935. By this time the extension from Woodseats to Meadowhead (as shown on the blinds) had been opened for seven years - but the picture was taken on Abbeydale Road South.

Below: The final batch of Standards comprised Nos 243-8 of 1936, built after the introduction of a new design, apparently to use up existing parts. Number **246** was another car waiting to depart for Fulwood in postwar years, in this case showing the distinctive diagonal style of the lettering on the side destination blind. *(G H F Atkins)*

Nether Edge Tramway Conversion

Above: Dramatic new deliveries in March 1934 were ten torque convertor Leyland TD3c double-deckers. In such a hilly city, these would have been viewed with high expectations. The bodies were locally-built highbridge 55-seaters by Cravens. Number **97** (**WJ 9097**) was photographed at the Town Hall, where it was attracting some attention. ***Below:*** The new buses had been purchased to replace trams on the relatively short Nether Edge route, where extensive track relaying would have been required. The last tram had run on Saturday 24th March, and No. **92** (**WJ 9092**) was photographed at Nether Edge, turning into Machon Bank Road to reach the terminus in this high-class suburb. *(Both: STA/BCVM)*

Nether Edge Tramway Conversion

Above: Another view at Nether Edge has the air of a cold and crisp Sunday with people in their Sunday best who had the leisure to stop and look. Number **94 (WJ 9094)** was actually only a short distance away from the Corporation's former tram depot and works where many trams had been built. In the period between 1911 and 1915 the expansion of the new depot and works at Queens Road saw the Nether Edge premises run down and closed. *Below:* A notable Sheffield landmark from 1740 onwards was St. Paul's church in Pinstone Street. The new Town Hall was built alongside and was completed in 1896. St. Paul's was described as 'severely classical' in style, and forms the background to this view of No. **90 (WJ 9090)** newly in service, probably on 25th March 1934, and two years before the church was demolished. *(Both: STA/BCVM)*

Livery Contrasts

Above: A substantial batch of Leyland Titanics arrived in 1935, with No. **131** (**AWE 331**) entering service in January snows. This B-fleet vehicle took the number of another six-wheeler, the Guy FCX shown on page 29. The Cravens 60-seat body was presented in a darker version of the blue and cream livery, as shown here. *(STA)* ***Below:*** Following several demonstration models, batches of AEC Regents were received regularly over a thirty year period. Sixteen arrived in 1935, including No. **232** (**BWA832**) with Weymann's body. These vehicles displayed the new light livery of cream with azure blue bands which was also adorning the new trams at this time.

A Dramatic Occasion

Richard Moore travelled on the last bus to the remote Derwent Village, and took photographs of the occasion prior to the flooding of the valley to create the Ladybower reservoir. This had been a long project, commencing when the Water Board obtained revised parliamentary powers in 1920. Sustained opposition at national level meant that construction did not start until 1935, but the properties - homes, church and Derwent Hall - survived until the task was nearing completion in 1943. The diversion of the bus service on 30th March that year is our best indication of the date of the photograph. The vehicle, with wartime hooded headlamps, was Leyland TD4c/Cravens No. **277** (**CWB 477**) of 1936, itself to be withdrawn after fire damage in 1945.

The Tilt Test

Above: Drama on a regular basis was played out at the manufacturer's when new buses were tilt-tested for stability. At the Weymann's factory in 1935, AEC Regent No. **101** (**BWA 201**) was performing satisfactorily. *Left:* At the Leyland factory three years later, the protractor had been thoughtfully emended to tell us the seating capacity of No. **381** (**EWJ 281**), a Titan TD5c. *(Lower picture: STA/BCVM)*

AEC Regents

Above: A more mundane occurrence was the taking of the official picture of No. **352** (**EWA 152**), a 1937 AEC Regent with Weymann's body.

Below: Similar vehicle No. **366** (**EWJ 466**) of 1938 was less than a year old when photographed in April 1939. The small lettering displays the name of General Manager H Watson, who was at the helm from 1936 to 1945. *(G H F Atkins)*

Styling Developments

Above: No Leyland-bodied vehicles had joined the fleet since 1933, and by the time No. **4** (**EWJ 304**) arrived in 1938 great advances in styling had been made. This TD5c was for the B fleet and carried the appropriate composite title. *(STA/BCVM)* **Below:** The Corporation's works at Queens Road had not built any bus bodies since 1925, but did produce a number on AEC Regent chassis over the years 1938-41. Number **410** (**GWB 510**) of 1939 had little if any of the stunning elegance of the Domed-roof tramcars in production at the same time.

Domed Roof Tramcars - 1

Above: The tramway to Millhouses had been extended south on reserved track to Beauchief in 1926, and thence via Abbey Lane to meet the Woodseats terminus in 1927. This Abbey Lane postwar view, a late date for one of Richard Moore's lantern slides, brings us to the new version of the standard Sheffield tramcar introduced in 1936. Number **249** was one of the first year's deliveries. *Below:* The modern domed roof made quite a contrast with the previous 'flat' roof. In this design it was coupled with smaller lower saloon windows, half-drop style, and with air vents instead of opening quarterlights. This is a late view of 1938 car No. **296** approaching the distinctive Locarno dance hall on London Road. *(John Lythgoe)*

Domed Roof Tramcars - 2

Above: Photographing the trams was difficult in the dark industrial districts of the city. Nevertheless No. **264** made a fine picture as it turned from Sheffield Road into Vulcan Road at Tinsley. The original striking appearance of these cars was muted when wartime blackout led to the cream roofs being painted dark grey. *Below:* The extension of the Firth Park route on to Barnsley Road at Sheffield Lane Top was made in 1934 and involved a dramatic steep curve out of Stubbin Lane. Car No. **298** of 1938 was negotiating the corner on the last day of the route in 1960. By this time, the car had been rebuilt with sliding windows. *(Both: John Lythgoe)*

The Second World War

No account of Sheffield's history could omit reference to the terrible German blitz on the city in December 1940. Two views of damage in the city centre are worth the proverbial thousand words, with the remains of car **274** *(above)* and car **231** *(below)*. To the right of 231, another car was almost obliterated. It had been No. 227 or 261. Altogether fourteen lost trams were replaced by new domed-roof cars in due course.

Wartime Expedients

Above: The tram fleet was augmented by 24 balcony cars from Newcastle and Bradford in 1941-43, rebuilt by Sheffield before entering service. An official photograph shows No. **311** (ex-Newcastle 122), which was one of the last to be withdrawn in 1952. This transfer led to the survival of one of them (317) as a hut, and its eventual restoration as Newcastle open-topper 114 at Beamish Museum in County Durham. *Below:* Numerous Guy and Daimler buses were received to wartime utility specification in the years 1943-46. One of them was No. **83** (**HWB 383**), a 1945 Daimler CWA6 with Duple body. This photograph in Barnsley Road at Osgathorpe Road in July 1946 was taken to demonstrate the unsuitable siting of the bus and tram stops at this point.

A Year of Jubilee

Above: The nation had plenty to celebrate with the end of the war in 1945, and in the same spirit the Department celebrated its own golden jubilee in 1946. Balcony car 353 of 1914 had been converted to a decorated car for the Silver Jubilee of King George V in 1935 and was also used for these later occasions. By the time of this 1946 "wedding cake" photograph outside Queens Road works the car had been renumbered **310.** It was scrapped in 1953, the year of the Coronation of Queen Elizabeth II. *Below:* A new tram numbered **501** was designed and built at the same works in 1946, and was appropriately named the Jubilee car, seen here posed on the turning circle at Millhouses for an official picture.

Pond Street Bus Station

Above: Opposite Midland Station a site for a bus station began to be provided from 1936. Some ten years later in the war-damaged city, the facility amounted only to two long platforms with rudimentary shelters. In this scene in Pond Street, tram **42** has prominence, with AEC Regent No. **407** (**FWA 907**) passing. At the far stances are Regent No. **308** and TD5c Titan No. **429** (**CWJ 408**, **GWE 729**), whilst in the centre Leyland/Cravens single-decker No. **156** (**FWJ 856**) proves to be too small for the queue. *Below:* A few moments later, freshly-painted No. **203** (**BWB 203**) draws up behind, and the waiting passengers surge towards it.

The Postwar Enthusiast

With astonishing rapidity we have absorbed the idea that worldwide information is immediately and universally available. We already need to be told that it was not always like that - so quick is our adaptation and so short are our memories. The point is made as I recall my first visit with a camera to see Sheffield's trams. How was I to know where to go and what to photograph?

My appetite had been whetted by Richard Wiseman's splendid articles in the attractive *Modern Tramway* magazine in 1957 and 1958. Armed with this and other information a year later, I knew that I would no longer be able to travel by tram to Darnall and Elm Tree, nor along the single track and loop line via Furnival Street in the city centre. Nevertheless, the rest of the system described in the articles still remained, and I set off on 18th March 1959 to travel the hundred miles to Sheffield where I would ride the trams and take some photographs. I particularly had my eye on the reserved track in Abbey Lane which connected Beauchief and Woodseats to create a great circular route in the city's southern suburbs.

Accordingly I emerged from Midland station, found the tram shelters in Pond Street and caught a tram via Chesterfield Road to Woodseats. The car was terminating here, so I got off and looked around. It was a major junction, with the lines continuing forward to Meadowhead and also turning right into Abbey Lane. I waited for a while for a tram along the reserved track, only to be eventually told that there weren't any. What a disappointment! This section of line had been abandoned just eighteen days earlier, and of course the news had not reached me. How could it have done? I had no personal friends or correspondents who might have been able to keep me up to date with tramway events in the city, and the closure, although reported as promptly as possible, was not in Modern Tramway until the April issue.

It was a very fine reserved track, on a gentle suburban lane with high quality houses and plenty of grass, trees and gardens, and a feeling that the country was not far away. This was the southern fringe of Sheffield, away from the industry and edging on to the delights of the Derbyshire moors. It represented the

city and its transport at their best. And what a city! World famous for its steel, particularly in cutlery and tools, this huge city of half a million people is spread across a whole range of hills gatherered round the two rivers whose valleys create the principal level sections. The River Sheaf, from which the city takes its name, comes from the south to join the Don which flows east to Rotherham, Doncaster, Goole and the sea. But the comic postcard could be cruel. One example was a very obvious fake depicting darkened factories with innumerable chimneys all pouring out smoke; it was captioned "Beautiful Sheffield" - and the publisher had the effrontery to publish the card in his "Real Photo" series.

If the reality was hard work and grime, and the image was unflattering, the spirit was not cowed. The city's trams and buses were built, presented and operated to the highest standards. In the first and second generations, that presentation was in an attractive dark blue and cream, but the style could be said to be typical of most tram and bus operators of the period. In 1935, in the midst of a massive fleet renewal programme, it was as if someone had said, "With standards like these, we should be doing more to show off the quality!" A new cream livery, smartly and simply trimmed in a lighter blue, took to the streets. This was revolutionary - fine for a seaside town of jollity and gaiety, but surely not in one of the biggest and most industrial of cities? It was a huge challenge deliberately undertaken, for these light coloured vehicles would show the dirt all too easily, but Sheffield rose to the challenge and kept them all clean and smart, lightening the city in the midst of its darkness.

In pre-war years the transport enthusiast and photographer was something of a rarity. Few could afford either the time or the money.

A handful of men whose names are now legend in transport circles travelled the country between 1920 and 1940 and took high quality photographs of trams and buses in many far flung places. The enthusiast historian owes them an incalculable debt. Others followed as the country gradually recovered from the second world war, but it was well into the nineteen-fifties before the activities of the enthusiast began to become commonplace. By then, even the greatest tramway undertakings were in decline, and they amassed a multitude of followers from all over the country and beyond. Only on special tour and Last Tram days would photographers be seen in hordes, but Sheffield with its central location was always easy to visit. The citizens would have been amazed had they known how many people in the course of a year were getting off trains at Victoria and Midland stations for the sole purpose of seeing the trams.

Once in the city, the interested observer could not fail to notice the Transport Department's bus fleet, large, very varied and full of interest. To start with, there was the distinctive phenomenon of the three separate sections, lettered A, B and C on the actual vehicles. Many an enthusiast had to work it out for himself, noticing the different fleetnames 'Transport' or 'Joint Omnibus Committee', and the variations in the legal ownership lettering including mention of the British Transport Commission. The vehicle variety began with the fact that there was no such thing as a standard Sheffield bus. The principal chassis manufacturers were AEC and Leyland, but just when you thought that they were standardising on one, the next order brought a large number of the other. There were smaller numbers of other makes such as Crossley and Daimler, the latter rising to renewed prominence in post-tramway days with the success of its Fleetline model.

The variety of chassis was as nothing compared to the range of coachbuilders patronised by the undertaking. The most distinctive was Eastern Coach Works because of the post-1948 restriction on availability outside the British Transport Commission. The BTC's membership of the Joint Committee opened the doors of this coachbuilder to the Sheffield B and C fleets, but the similar opportunity to purchase Bristol chassis was not taken up in those days. Local bus builders were patronised, the obvious contenders being the Sheffield firm of Cravens, and Charles Roberts of Horbury near Wakefield. A little further afield and significant at national level was Charles H Roe of Leeds, extensively patronised by Sheffield, as was Weymann's of Addlestone, Surrey, and Leyland. Post-war exigencies saw bus bodies also purchased from Cawood, Crossley, Mann Egerton, Northern Coachbuilders, Strachan and Wilkes & Meade, and a later period saw additions from Alexander, Burlingham, Park Royal, East Lancashire and Neepsend. The last-named built buses locally in Penistone Road to East Lancashire's designs but under Cravens ownership.

The Sheffield fleet thus contained a degree of interest unparallelled elsewhere, and the most avid tram enthusiast was likely to have his head turned by the remarkable variety of the city's buses. The livery also permitted of numerous variations in a manner not found in other comparable large fleets. Such elements as cream or grey roofs, blue bands or blue window surrounds, cream, blue or half-and-half bonnet panels - all these would be standardised in most places, but in Sheffield were different from batch to batch, within batches, or before and after repaints.

Keeping on top of developments in such a fleet was a task only really possible for the local observer, coming and going in the city every day. One such was John Lythgoe, who was particularly active in the years 1958-64, and thus covered with his camera the last years of the trams and the ever-interesting progress of the bus fleet. Whilst Richard Moore's archive has brought to light a variety of items not seen before, it has, as stated earlier, also given us the opportunity to see some familiar pictures to better advantage. In the case of John Lythgoe's pictures, they form the greater part of the presentation of the years 1948-74 with the added bonus that they have not previously been published. They are, however, augmented by views from the legendary Geoffrey Atkins as well as by some from my own camera, and a number of the later views from Richard Moore also find a place here.

So we set out once again, this time mostly with John Lythgoe as our guide. The change of emphasis from professional to enthusiast will be noticed. It enables the book as a whole to paint a picture in many varied hues.

Postwar Renewal

Above: Peacetime double-deck deliveries resumed in the spring of 1947 with AEC Regents bodied by Weymann's. Brand new No. **527** (**JWB 727**) was loading at one of the bus station's outside stances in the inappropriately named Flat Street leading up the hill into Fitzalan Square. Wartime Daimler No. **82** (**HWB 382**) on the right carried a Duple body. *(G H F Atkins)*

Below: The next batch had sliding window ventilators and outswept lower deck panelling, as seen here on No. **559** (**JWE 859**). The location is Psalter Lane at the Methodist Church and the adjacent Montessori School in April 1960.

Postwar Renewal

Above: The portly conductor would find fare collection on AEC Regent No. **568** (**JWE 868**) hard work at busy times, with the 7ft 6ins vehicle width then prevailing. A short break gives him time to relax briefly. *(G H F Atkins)*

Below: A very different type to join the fleet in the summer of 1947 was the Crossley-bodied Crossley single-decker, of which there were six. Number **241** (**JWJ 741**) was in the A fleet but was photographed at Baslow on the 37 to Bakewell, which was a Joint Committee C route into the Peak District. *(Robert F Mack)*

Amazing Variety

Above: The interest engendered by the postwar Sheffield bus fleet is perfectly illustrated by this 1953 line-up of five vehicles of 1948-49 displaying the work of five coachbuilders and three chassis manufacturers. At the far left is AEC/Weymann's No. **184** (**KWJ 184**) next to all-Leyland No. **38** (**KWE 438**). In the middle is Crossley No. **592** (**KWB 92**) bodied by Northern Coachbuilders, followed by all-Crossley No. **598** (**LWB 298**) in 1952 green livery. At far right is No. **108** (**KWJ 808**), a Roberts-bodied AEC. (*G H F Atkins*)

Left: The previous style of postwar Crossley body lacked the drooping window corners of the well-known Manchester version, but the windscreen still gave a hint of it, as seen on No. **575** (**KWA 775**), also on Crossley chassis.

Single-deckers

Above: The Weymann's-bodied Leyland PS1 entered the fleet from 1947 and was closely related to London Transport's TD class. The official Weymann's picture shows No. **176** (**KWA 276**) prior to delivery.

Below: Number **218** (**KWA 218**) was built to the same 34-seat specification, and was seen on Ecclesall Road opposite Endcliffe Park on Whit Sunday morning in 1960. This was another example of a Corporation A fleet bus operating a Joint Committee service, in this case as far as Calver Sough on the B route 40.

Leyland Coachwork

Above: The postwar Leyland body also entered the fleet from 1947, and was an obvious adaptation of the classic prewar style. The first batch included No. **543** (**KWA 543**), seen entering Pond Street bus station in September 1963.

Below: Delivery of the large second batch was spread over several months in 1948 and included No. **271** (**KWE 871**). There was nothing unusual about the operation of buses on Boxing Day in 1960 when this picture was taken in Psalter Lane on a service 4 journey to Bents Green.

More Single Deckers

Above: Many more Leyland PS1 single-deckers came in 1948, including the distinctively-registered No. **201** (**KWE 1**) for the C fleet. The picture was taken during a pause at The Snake Inn on route 48 for Manchester on 2nd July 1960. Modellers might note that the roof has a central darker area, probably painted 'smudge' - a greyish mixture of Sheffield's azure blue and cream.

Below: A more pug-like appearance marked the AEC Regals, created by the shorter mudguards and more blunt radiator styling, although the Weymann's body is the same on both vehicles. Our example is No. **1181** (**KWJ 181**), originally 181, at Buxton in April 1956. *(G H F Atkins)*

Roberts Coachwork

The railway wagon company Charles Roberts was an active bus builder in the postwar years. This AEC Regent No. **322 (KWB 922)** of 1948 was one of those in the Sheffield fleet, followed by new trams in the style of the Jubilee car 501 from the same works in 1950-52. This Pond Street scene also shows up the inadequacy of the passenger shelters at the time. *(Richard Moore)*

More Roberts Coachwork

Above: Number **334** (**KWB 934**) had arrived in the autumn of 1948. When this photograph was taken some fifteen years later at one of the outside stances in Pond Street, it included the bus station buildings which had been significantly developed from 1954. *Below:* An earlier scene inside the bus station, in 1951, showed No. **122** (**LWA 22**), another Roberts-bodied AEC Regent. The much older vehicle in the background was the Department's mobile staff canteen which was in use from 1943 to 1958. This was registered **VO 7445** and had been converted from a Leyland-bodied Lion LT3 bus acquired from the War Department. *(G H F Atkins)*

Crossley and Cravens

Above: This fascinating line-up was photographed at Bramall Lane with the generous co-operation of garage staff one evening in August 1959. Nearest the camera is No. **598 (LWB 298)**, a 1949 all-Crossley vehicle originally ordered by Liverpool Corporation, and No. **599 (LWB 299)** of the same batch is beside it. The revised body style had a neater appearance than the previous version, exemplified by the third vehicle which is No. **580 (KWA 780)**. An unidentified Roberts-bodied AEC Regent III completed the quartet, and Bramall Lane garage closed at the end of July 1963.

Below: A batch of AEC Regents with Cravens bodies came in 1949-50. The August fields provided a backdrop for the Cravens photographer to snap No. **231 (LWB 831)**, the first one to be delivered.

A London Connection

The Cravens bodies bore a strong resemblance to RT-type buses built for London Transport, but sliding windows were specified by Sheffield. These can be seen in the view of No. **246 (LWB 746)** *(above)* at work in Pond Street bus station *(G H F Atkins)*, as well as in the official interior shot of No. **231** *(below)*, showing a design that was light and airy and distinctively Sheffield.

Towards Standardisation - 1

A livery variation which became characteristic of the Leyland Farington style of body had blue window surrounds, and large numbers of the type were received on the PD2 chassis. This picturesque view of No. **1144 (LWE 144)** was taken from Limb Lane at Whirlow on route 50 (City - Dore via Brocco Bank) in May 1963.

Towards Standardisation - 2

Above: This typical Leyland PD2/1 with 'Farington' body entered service with a cream roof in 1949 but is seen here in the first-overhaul livery as applied in the R C Moore period (1945-61). Number **628** (**LWJ 628**) was in Burngreave Road approaching Burngreave Vestry Hall on 28th September 1962.

Below: The new General Manager from 1961 was C T Humpidge, who introduced some livery changes. As you look at this view of No. **625** (**LWJ 625**) in Fitzalan Square in December 1965, note that the roof has reverted to cream, and there is black paint between the front destination displays. *(Author)*

The Mobile Library

Above and below: Another distinctive body order was that placed with Strachans for eight single-deckers on Leyland PS2/1 chassis, delivered in 1950. Number **56** (**MWA 756**) was notable for being converted to a mobile library in 1962, as shown in these pictures taken shortly afterwards. The livery closely followed the Department's bus fleet standard, but with appropriate changes for Sheffield City Libraries ownership.

Northern Coachbuilders

Above: Several detail alterations made the Northern Coachbuilders bodies on 1950 AEC Regents noticeably different from earlier examples. Number **429** (**MWA 829**) was seen entering Pond Street bus station in September 1963. The dramatic backcloth of Park Hill flats graced many photographs of this period. This housing showpiece was an example of the 'homes for the future' but quickly degenerated into an area of social problems. *Below:* Later livery variations included black paint added between the front destination displays, cream lower bonnet side and red (previously black) wheel centres. However, it was the cream roof that made the most noticeable difference to No. **432** (**MWA832**).

The Roberts Tramcars

Whilst the bus fleet was being extensively renewed after the war, the trams were still hard at work carrying the majority of the passengers. These two views from Richard Moore's archive give particular prominence to the overhead, and notably feature two of the 35 new trams built by Roberts and delivered in 1950-52. *Above:* Against the new C & A store built on the site of the one lost by bombing in 1940, car **527** in High Street at Fitzalan Square was working to Tinsley (Vulcan Road). *Below:* Car **518** bound for the same destination was pictured in the gentle setting of Abbey Lane.

Leyland Olympic

Above: The underfloor-engined single-decker was a radical development which made an early appearance in Sheffield. The integrally contructed Leyland Olympic was bodied by Weymann's, who took this picture of No. **228** (**NWA 928**) at their factory in February 1951. The 44-seater was a notable advance on the existing 34-seaters, and entered service the following month. *Below*: There were four of the type in the Sheffield fleet, and in September 1963 No. **226** (**NWA 926**) was seen entering Pond Street bus park.

Mann Egerton Speciality

A great rarity was the Mann Egerton double deck body, of which there were two on Leyland PD2/12 chassis, dating from the spring of 1952. The first of them was No. **361 (NWE 561)**, seen on Platform B in Pond Street bus station in 1960. The inset destination display and the damaged front dome are worthy of note, as is the addition of the offside front trafficator carried on a built-up housing.

Timeless Elegance

Whilst the Roberts tramcars were still being delivered, the City Council decided on a long-term programme of tramway closures. The first of them took place with the last tram to Fulwood via Hunter's Bar on 5th January 1952. Particularly graceful lines marked the replacing buses, Sheffield's first to the new eight feet width, with classically-styled Roe bodies on Leyland chassis. They featured the patented Roe safety staircase and window, and these pictures show the effect of two different livery styles. Number **392** (**NWE 592**) *(above)* was in Burngreave Road in 1962, and No. **393** (**NWE 593**) *(below, by the author)* was at the Bridge Street city centre terminus in 1965.

Old Faithfuls Rebodied

The two 1938 A E C Regents shown on this page were among a number to receive new Roe bodies, in this case in June 1952. In that year extensive trials of a green livery were in progress, some vehicles two-tone but others in one shade with no relief of any kind. The plain version is illustrated by No. **407** (**FWA 907**) in Pond Street bus station. The repainting in standard fleet livery some eighteen months later was much welcomed, and No. **403** (**FWA 903**) was pictured subsequently in Penistone Road. *(G H F Atkins; Robert F Mack)*

More Leyland Bodies

Above: Further Leyland bodies appeared on a batch of PD2/10 Titans in 1952. They were to the neater style associated with the final design from Leyland, but in this case to the 7ft 6ins width. They had the added distinction, if it can be called that, of being delivered in the experimental green livery, but No. **659 (OWB 859)** was photographed after first overhaul in cream with dark grey 'smudge' roof and blue window surrounds. The 169 route number refers to a variation on the Sheffield to Rotherham joint bus service which had replaced the last of Rotherham's trams in 1948. *Below:* As with other types, the later cream roof and the black paint between destination boxes made a notable improvement, exemplified on No. **667 (OWB 867)** entering Pond Street bus station in 1963.

A New Standard

New AEC Regents with coachwork by Charles H Roe first entered the fleet in 1952, and such vehicles were to play a significant part in the massive tram-replacement programme which was already under way. *Above:* The attractive lines were shown to advantage when No. **19 (OWE 19)** was photographed in Pond Street bus station. *(G H F Atkins)* ***Below:*** An action shot in The Moor caught No. **114 (OWE 114)** on route 59 to Bradway in June 1960, by which time the tram service had been so reduced that no car was in sight.

Before Park Hill Flats

This splendid group again illustrates the variety which created such interest in the Sheffield bus fleet, in a scene dating from April 1953. In the centre is No. **119 (OWE 119)**, another of the 1952 AEC Regents, with 1953 Leyland No. **157 (PWA 257)** on the right. The row of older buses parked behind includes a 1941 AEC Regent bodied by the Corporation itself, in this case No. **424 (GWE 624)**. The skyline behind the Midland Station is equally varied. (*G H F Atkins*)

Coronation Year - 1

Above: Early deliveries in 1953 were Weymann's 58-seaters on Leyland PD2/12 chassis. This one is No. **148** (**PWA 248**), photographed in May 1960 at Nether Edge terminus in Union Road, adjacent to Nether Edge Hospital. The bus had arrived here on service 61 but was ready to depart as a 98 to Southey Green via Longley Lane. The exterior advertisement is by Cowan-Ad, hand-painted in the Queens Road workshop.

Below: Renumbering of much of the B fleet in 1963 meant that No. 158 (**PWA 258**) had become **2158** by the time of this photograph taken by the author in Commercial Street in 1964.

Coronation Year - 2

Above: Later arrivals in 1953 were AEC Regents with Roe bodies, and No. **176** (**RWA 176**) makes a fine study at Pond Street bus station. *(G H F Atkins).*

Below: A later study in the same vicinity shows No. **177** (**RWA 177**) in May 1960 ready to work route 59 to Bradway, with tram lines and overhead still in evidence although by this date this section was not in normal service use.

Coronation Year - 3

Above: Dramatic new arrivals from Weymann's in 1953 were two saloons on the heavy Leyland Royal Tiger chassis. The bodies had standee accommodation, and a corner entrance style more particularly associated with Edinburgh. With three steps needed to reach the platform, the resemblance to an ordinary double-decker was faint indeed, and the whole arrangement was of concern to the local vehicle inspectorate. Number **223** (**RWA 223**) was photographed by the coachbuilder before delivery.

Below: It was almost a year later when the pair finally entered service, after the fitment of a rear emergency door as shown in this view of No. **222** (**RWA 222**) at Pond Street. These vehicles were invariably to be found on service 31 from City to Walkley Lane via Upperthorpe.

Tramway Replacement

Above: Following the 1952 programme, a further small rebodying exercise took place in 1953. One of the four utility vehicles to receive new Roe bodies was Daimler CWD6 No. **518** (**HWB 508**) of 1945. In this scene it is outside Leadmill Road garage in March 1959. *(G H F Atkins)*

Below: By contrast, a large scale event was the replacement of the Ecclesall - City - Middlewood tram service on 28th March 1954. Number **695** (**RWJ 695**) was one of the substantial number of Leyland PD2/12 with Weymann's bodies purchased for this task, and seen at Ecclesall terminus in April 1961.

AEC Regents of 1954

Above: Significant numbers of AEC Regents with Weymann's bodies also arrived in 1954. The design had changed subtly from that of the previous year, and the coachbuilder's own photograph depicts No. **734 (SWE 434)**. **Below:** The type is also represented by No. **729 (SWE 429)** at Pond Street. In both pictures, the substantial semaphore type trafficator is worthy of note. The flashing type was to become standard within the next couple of years, at first often at only the front of the vehicle. *(G H F Atkins)*

AEC Regents of 1954

It is detailed differences which often provide interest for the observer. *Above:* The semaphore trafficator was still in situ on No. **191 (SWE 291)** but changes governing the position of rear lights had resulted in an extended lamp housing on the platform which is particularly clear in this view. *(Richard Moore)*

Below: By the time of this June 1963 picture of No. **725 (SWE 425)**, flashing trafficators had been fitted. At the Eyre Street and Bramall Lane roundabout, note also the relaxed group of gentlemen passing the time of day at the corner of Cumberland Street, and the road signs to Worksop and Newark provided by the RAC rather than by the highway authority

AEC Regents of 1954

Taking a further look at detailed features, the rear view of **SWE 297** clearly shows us the extended
lamp housing and the slightly untidy arrangement of the lamps and reflectors. The distinctive shape
of the emergency window with its inlet opening handle was a Weymann's feature found in many
fleets. This particular vehicle had recently been renumbered from 197 to **2197** when this picture was
taken in 1963.

The AEC Monocoach

Above: Four years after the integrally constructed Leyland Olympic, a small number of the comparable Monocoach from AEC and Park Royal arrived in 1955. The manufacturer's photograph of No. **1205** (**TWJ 505**) prior to delivery shows the more comfortable seats fitted for use on the C fleet's long services. *Below:* Halfway through the comparatively short life of this batch in Sheffield, No. **1203** (**TWJ 503**) was photographed in 1960. The older vehicles alongside were AEC No. **263** on the right and Leyland No. **385** on the left.

Concealed Radiators

Above: Nineteen fifty-five was a quiet year but enlivened by the striking modernity (as it seemed to the young observer) of the new concealed-radiator styling. The first of the type in the Sheffield fleets was a batch of Roe-bodied AEC Regents, and No. **1258** (**UWE 758**) was pictured in Castlegate. *(G H F Atkins)*

Below: Whit Sunday morning in 1960 saw No. **739** (**VWJ 539**) of the A fleet leaving the city for the rural run to Castleton on the 72 route. The scene is at Endcliffe Park on Ecclesall Road.

For Tramway Replacement

Above: A substantial further number of AEC Regents with Roe bodies had arrived by the spring of 1956 for the conversion of another intensive cross-city tramway service, with the last trams running between Walkley and Intake on 7th April. By the time of this 1962 photograph of No. **737** (**VWJ 537**) on Gower Street at Ellesmere Road, the livery had been significantly lightened.

Below: The alternative livery style graced similar B fleet vehicle No. **1269** (**UWE 769**) at the time of this photograph in July 1965. *(G H F Atkins)*

Styling Contrasts

Above: Further AEC Regents delivered later in 1956 had Weymann's bodies. In this picture of No. **778** (**WWB 778**) the photographer was recording the contrast with the Roe body on No. **1276** (**VWE 76**).The Orion styling of No. 778 had originated with Weymann's Metro-Cammell associate some two years earlier and presented a much more stark appearance than the 1954 deliveries to Weymann's own designs. The shallow upper saloon windows contributed significantly to the 'bald' look.

Below: A second contrast created in 1956 was of lowbridge and highbridge versions of the Orion body. This is illustrated by highbridge No. **748** (**WWB 748**) caught on camera next to lowbridge No. **1286** (**WWB 486**) in August 1956. *(Both: G H F Atkins)*

The Low Bridge Problem

Above: The low height buses were required for service under Anston railway bridge in the hard-fought territory east of the city. The formidable adversary thirty years before had been the United-controlled W T Underwood Ltd, later East Midland. The 1956 delivery consisted of nine vehicles, and **1291 (WWB 491)** was officially posed for Richard Moore's camera.

Below: Number **1285 (WWB 485)** was seen entering Pond Street bus station on service 19 from Dinnington in 1962. The roadway beneath the offending railway bridge was subsequently lowered to permit the operation of highbridge buses.

Trams in the Fifties - 1

To tell the story of the 1950s only in terms of new vehicles would be to lose sight of the continuing presence of the trams on some of the busiest routes.

Above: Standard car **208** was gingerly negotiating track repairs on the Sheffield Lane Top route at Fir Vale, with the red flag as a warning to other road users.

Below: The "Tram Pinch" sign at Owlerton served to support the author's bicycle as well as to warn motorists of a narrowing of the space between track and kerb. Domed-roof tram No. **233** and a parked car demonstrated the point. *(Both: Author)*

Trams in the Fifties - 2

The wartime replacement cars built between 1941 and 1944 all had sliding window openers from new, and two are shown here.

Above: Car No. **100** and a Standard were at Meadowhead terminus on the A61 trunk road to Chesterfield. *Below:* Under two miles away was Beauchief, a stub terminus in 1959-60 after the closure of the Abbey Lane route, where No. **483** was seen in the trams' last winter. Both routes served attractive residential areas.

Trams in the Fifties - 3

These scenes illustrate the care with which the terminus at Sheffield Lane Top was designed. It occupied a wide part of the road, and an island with a passenger shelter was built alongside the terminal stub. Road traffic could pass unimpeded whilst passengers were sheltered and protected. The installation was completed by a trolley reverser. The triangle of overhead wire was a familiar sight throughout the city and made for speedy and convenient reversals.

Above: Car **256** was in the act of negotiating the reverser as it set off for the city. *Below:* The view in the opposite direction, taken from the passenger shelter, showed car No. **296** retreating apace.

Tramway Replacement

Above: Nineteen fifty-seven was an ominous year for the tramways, the closure of another major cross-city service reducing the system to about half of what it once had been. Huge orders for new buses brought 40 more AEC Regents with Weymann's bodies and the last trams ran between Crookes and Handsworth on 4th May. This 1963 photograph shows No. **807** (**XWJ 807**) at Pond Street bus station.

Below: Another huge order brought 40 Leyland PD2/20 with Roe bodies. In this view No. **842** (**YWA 842**) from that order, on the left, can be compared with the following year's **517** (**4517 WB**) at the Barnsley Road turning circle at Sheffield Lane Top in April 1959.

An Eastern Coach Works Surprise

Above: Five Leyland PD2/20 chassis carrying Eastern Coach Works bodies created quite a stir among enthusiasts when they arrived in 1957. The body style was similar to that on the last Bristol KSW types being delivered to Bristol and Brighton & Hove at the same time. This is the manufacturer's view of **1152** (**YWB 152**).

Below: Number **1153** (**YWB 153**) had been fitted with platform doors by the time of this December 1965 photograph, a time of year when they would have been particularly welcome. The bus was arriving at Pond Street after a trip to Retford, the limit of double-deck working on the long 85 service. *(Author)*

Works Service

Above: Some minor tramway closures were little publicised and are now almost forgotten. One such was the industrial service from City to Sheffield Lane Top via Attercliffe, making use of a line in Newhall Road and running for the last time on 26th October 1957. Similar services via Brightside, Upwell Street and Owler Lane had all ceased by the end of February 1959, and 1957 Leyland PD2/30 No. **487** (**4487 WB**) with Weymann's body was photographed on a replacement service at Sheffield Lane Top in April 1959. The destination "Hawke Street" indicated a short working to the end of Upwell Street.

Below: On the opposite side of the city, No. **495** (**4495 WB**) of the same batch was on ordinary service at Woodhouse railway station on a wintry day in 1965. *(Author)*

Contrasts in 1958

Above: The principal tramway closure in 1958 was of Staniforth Road and the two-mile reserved track in Prince of Wales Road, reached via Attercliffe and served for the last time on 12th April. One of the twenty replacing buses was No. **501** (**4501 WB**), a Roe-bodied Leyland PD2/30 seating 59. It was photographed in Fitzalan Square some time in the 1960s passing the same spot where we saw tram No. 1 in 1899 on page 16. *(Richard Moore)*

Below: A most impressive vehicle to arrive in May 1958 was AEC Reliance No. **900** (**9000 WB**), with Roe 'Dalesman' 37-seat coach body. It was an extravagance provided mainly for the use of the Transport Committee, although also used for private hire work, and was found parked in Psalter Lane in June 1959.

Solving the low bridge problem?

During the 1958-59 winter six AEC Bridgemaster buses not only introduced the low-floor low-height double-decker to the Sheffield fleet, but also the high capacity bus built to the now-permitted length of thirty feet. The rather ungainly Park Royal bodies seated 76. These two views at the Herdings terminus in the south of the city on 20th August 1961 show *(above)* the front view of No. **524 (2524 WE)**, and *(below)* the rear aspect of No. **522 (2522 WE)**.

Mastering a bridge

AEC Bridgemaster No. **523 (2523 WE)** was leaving Pond Street bus station for Gleadless, also in the south of the city, when photographed waiting to emerge from Pond Hill into Sheaf Street. The bus is standing on the bridge over the River Sheaf, and the spire of St. Marie's church completes a splendidly composed picture. (*G H F Atkins*)

The Ravages of Redevelopment

Above: Leyland PD2/30 No. **1161** (**3161 WE**) had a 59-seat Roe body with platform doors for long distance routes such as the 37 to Bakewell shown here. The scene was on The Moor in September 1960, with attendant road works for redevelopment at Moorhead which included a short temporary monorail system for the contractor's use. Across the road, notices in the former premises of Roberts Brothers announce the removal of their department store to the newly-built Rockingham House, further down The Moor.

Below: The nearby St. Mary's Gate presented a rather bleak scene in June 1963 when No. **907** (**3907 WE**) of 1959 was making use of the redeveloped roadway. The bus itself was a Leyland PD3/1 at first sight the same as 1161 above, but in fact thirty-feet long and seating 69 passengers.

Contrasts in 1959

Above: The medium-weight Leyland Leopard chassis made its appearance in the summer of 1959 in the Sheffield fleet in a batch of six with Weymann's 'Fanfare' coach bodies. They typically operated the lengthy rural services, and in this scene No. **1304 (1504 WJ)** had arrived at Pond Street from Bakewell. *(G H F Atkins)*

Below: Another new type followed in the autumn when 25 Leyland Atlanteans replaced the trams which ran for the last time between Wadsley Bridge and Woodseats on 3rd October. The next day saw service 53 and bus No. **365 (665 WJ)** both brand new when this picture was taken. The Metro-Cammell body seated 78 and the thirty-feet length was now firmly established as the standard for the future fleet.

Eclipsing the Trams

Left: Replacement buses usually had to have different terminal arrangements from the trams, and this view shows the Woodseats terminus in Abbey Lane in August 1962 with No. **883** (**883 WJ**).

Below: The tramway in Pond Street remained intact to provide access to Queen's Road works during the last year of operation. The bus station is in the distance in this view of Atlantean No. **365** (**665 WJ**) in February 1960. *(G H F Atkins)*

A New Decade

Above: The year 1960 opened with the arrival of further Leyland Leopards with Weymann's coach bodies. The location here is Piccadilly, Manchester, where No. **1172 (6172 WJ)** had arrived from Sheffield on service 48 via The Snake on 2nd July that year. Alongside is Manchester Corporation's No. 4077 (GVR 379), a Brush-bodied Daimler of 1947 with distinctive Manchester styling.

Below: After several years of Leyland dominance, Sheffield's new deliveries in 1960 were mostly from AEC, who supplied 71 long Regent V models with three makes of body. The January arrivals included **1332 (6332 WJ)** with Roe body complete with platform doors. *(Author)*

Buses for Trams - 1

Above: More of the same batch came in April when No. **1345 (6345 WJ)** was seen in Low Edges Road a few days after entering service. These views emphasise the effect created by the livery variant applied to the Roe bodies, where the window surrounds were painted blue.

Below: Number **437 (7437 WJ)** was one of the Regents bodied by Weymann's to replace the trams between Sheffield Lane Top and Meadowhead on 3rd April 1960, and was seen at Meadowhead on the first day of service 75.

After the trams had gone, the new buses spread to other routes. Number **458 (7458 WJ)** of the Weymann's-bodied AEC Regents was in Psalter Lane near Sharrow Head when photographed in May 1961. Note the front wings with radiused lower edges - the chassis with Alexander bodies delivered at the same period in 1960 had wings with straight lower edges, although their chassis numbers were, in many cases, intermixed.

Buses for Trams - 3

Further views of the large batch of these AEC Regents bodied by Weymann's show numbers **448** (**7448 WJ**) and **443** (**7443 WJ**) at Sheffield Lane Top. The view *above* is at the same spot as the tram terminus, and the other is at the bus turning circle a little further on. *(Richard Moore; Author)*

Buses for Trams - 4

Above: The Alexander body was a new departure for Sheffield but the 25 Regents of April 1960 must have given good service because the coachbuilder received several repeat orders. Number **869 (7869 WJ)** was at Sheffield Lane Top on the same occasion as the previous picture. *(Author)*

Below: The same bus appears in another of those amazingly varied gatherings at which Sheffield was so good. As No. 869 had been new in April 1960 and AEC Regal No. **112 (KWJ 196)** on the far left was sold in the September, there can be no doubt about the year of the photograph. *(G H F Atkins)*

Buses for Trams - 5

Above: Even in Sheffield, where the tramway was so well run, the appearance en masse of the new replacing buses made a strong impression, exemplified by No. **878** (**7878 WJ**) at Meadowhead in April 1960.

Below: At a later date, this view of No. **873** (**7873 WJ**) outside the Booking Hall of Sheffield United Tours in Pond Street emphasised the length of these buses. *(G H F Atkins)*

Burlingham Coaches

Above: The description "Burlingham coach" usually brings to mind the perfect proportions of the classic 'Seagull' model, but for Sheffield in the summer of 1960 it meant a comfortably seated vehicle adapted from the manufacturer's service-bus designs. Number **1176** (**5876 W**) was a 41-seater on Leyland Leopard L1 chassis, and was photographed in front of the City Hall in July 1961.

Below: In between lengthy ordinary service runs, No. **1306** (**5906 W**) was seen waiting in Pond Street bus station. *(G H F Atkins)*

The End of the Trams - 1

Above: With the junctions gone, this view at the bottom of The Moor makes an interesting comparison with the 1898 scene on page 15. The heavy traffic congestion and preponderance of buses suggest 1960, with Standard tram No. **167** running through the roundabout to Millhouses on the last remaining route. The car itself has the rebuilt lower saloon with smaller windows.

Below: The presence of a tram with an Alexander-bodied bus dates this picture between April and October 1960. The tram is wartime No. **112**, turning from Fargate into High Street bound for Vulcan Road on the only remaining route. The Church Street tracks in the foreground remained intact as part of a useful avoiding triangle but carried no regular service. *(Both: Richard Moore archive)*

The End of the Trams - 2

Above: Some of the ancillary vehicles were retained to assist with the dismantling of the tramway. The AEC tower wagon **CWJ 410** had a lot of work ahead when photographed from tram 526 on Burngreave Road at Christ Church Road on the last day of trams to Sheffield Lane Top. This vehicle was originally bus 310 of 1937 and later served as a tree lopper before passing to the Tramway Museum Society in 1969.

Below: Throughout the final tramway years, dismantling activity could be observed at the Tinsley yard of T W Ward. The top deck of car **199** was moving for the last time when pictured in 1959. *(Author)*

The End of the Trams - 3

Above: Although it was quiet when compared with today's impossible situations, the growth in motor traffic in the 1960s was a serious problem for transport operators, and had no little influence on the demise of the trams. The situation was well illustrated in this view of car No. **254** in High Street in February 1960.

Below: As the end approached, the tram turning circle on reserved track at Millhouses was removed and replaced by one for buses. The trams latterly reversed on the adjacent crossover, as seen here with car No. **231** being witnessed by several enthusiasts on the last Sunday of operation.

The End of the Trams - 4

Above: Number **507** with less than a week to go was only about a third of the way through the expected normal life of such a car. It was standing between shifts in the shadow of Hadfield's steel works in Vulcan Road on 3rd October 1960, looking as well cared for as ever.

Below: Two Roberts cars were exquisitely decorated for the last week of the trams, and one of them was No. **513**, seen here in Abbeydale Road. The other was No. 510 and both took part in the final procession in pouring rain on Saturday 8th October and were then preserved.

The All-Bus Era

Above: Neither the Leyland Atlantean nor any other type ever made a clean sweep in the Sheffield fleet, but it was this model which eventually replaced the trams. In this scene under The Wicker arches after the roadway had been reinstated, the two 1960 Atlanteans are Nos **923** and **929** (**5923/9 W**) in the company of Rotherham Crossley No. **214** (**HET 514**). *(Richard Moore)*

Left: In the same way as "revised" fares means "increased", "revised" destination displays in this period were usually reduced. In a welcome move in the opposite direction the Metro-Cammell bodies on this batch had full rear displays as shown here on No. **918** (**5918 W**) at Woodseats terminus in Abbey Lane in August 1962. A step was provided for the conductor to reach the handles.

Left: On the same occasion as the previous picture, John Lythgoe produced this fine portrait of No. **920** (**5920 W**), another of the 1960 batch of Atlanteans which replaced the last trams.

Below: The standard Weymann's bus body pattern had shown little change since the remarkable Olympic design of 1951. In this example the body was mounted on a Leyland Leopard chassis, and No. **207** (**6307 W**) was delivered in the summer of 1960. *(G H F Atkins)*

Eastern Coach Works Speciality

After the huge additions to the bus fleet over several years, 1961 was quiet, but the nine vehicles delivered were of particular interest. The C fleet received five Leyland Leopards with bodies by Eastern Coach Works to a design usually found on the Bristol MW chassis.

Above: In its first month of service, No. **1181 (1881 WA)** was photographed on Ecclesall Road South near the Ecclesall terminus. *Below:* Number **1310 (1910 WA)** was in front of Sheffield City Hall when pictured in July that year.

A Unique Bridgemaster
Following the six rear-entrance AEC Bridgemasters of 1959, a 72-seat forward-entrance example arrived in 1961 but remained unique in the Sheffield fleet.

Right: This fine portrait of No. **525** (**1925 WA**) was taken at Herdings terminus on 20th August 1961.

Below: The ungainly lines of the Park Royal body are displayed in this picture in Sheaf Street outside the Midland station, as No. 525 was returning from Arbourthorne on service 105.

Park Royal and Metro-Cammell

Above: The delivery of four Park Royal-bodied Leyland Leopards in 1962 heralded an era in which this coachbuilder rose to considerable prominence in the Sheffield fleets. The typical BET Group style made an interesting contrast with the BTC style of the previous year's coaches. Numbers **11** and **13** (**615/7 BWB**) were photographed in 1971 on the forecourt of Herries Road garage, built on the north side of the city in 1952.

Below: Meanwhile, further Metro-Cammell Atlanteans were also arriving, and No. **939** (**939 BWB**) was seen at Woodhouse in 1965. *(Author)*

Leyland and Daimler

Above: The Roe-bodied Atlantean of 1962 was very similar to the Metro-Cammell design yet subtly different, and is shown on No. **947 (947 BWB)** in Fitzalan Square in 1965, working the former tram route to Prince of Wales Road.

Below: The first Daimler Fleetlines came 1962, with just three vehicles, but the type eventually came to oust the AEC Regent as the undertaking's alternative to Leyland. With Metro-Cammell body, No. **951 (951 BWB)** was at the Crookes terminus at Heavygate Avenue on a cold winter's night in 1968. *(Both: Author)*

AEC Regents

The many remaining vehicles which from 1947 had constituted large scale fleet renewal after the depredations of war were themselves in need of replacement from 1962 onwards. The huge tramway abandonment programme was therefore only just nicely completed when further substantial expenditure was called for.

Above: The little bus station at Bridge Street accommodated certain services to the north, and is seen here with No. **1362 (362 EWE)**, a 70-seat Park Royal-bodied AEC Regent of 1963. (*Author*)

Below: Similar machines Nos **73** and **65 (973/65 FWJ)** were photographed in Harmer Lane coming into the Pond Street station. *(G H F Atkins)*

AEC Regents

Above: Delivery of the AEC Regents continued into 1964, and in this view of **1150 (350 HWE)** the forward entrance layout is shown to advantage. *(G H F Atkins)*

Below: No. **1368 (368 HWE)** was loading in the village at Chapeltown in 1965 and would work inwards to the Bridge Street bus station in the city. The one forward entrance Bridgemaster had not found favour, and although the full-height equivalent proved successful, this batch proved to be the last front-engined buses for the undertaking. *(Author)*

Daimler Fleetlines

Above: A new style of Park Royal body made quite a stir when it appeared on a large batch of Daimler Fleetlines in 1964, and was immortalised in a cream-painted Matchbox model. Members of The Omnibus Society attending the Presidential Weekend hosted by Mr Humpidge in 1967 all received one as a souvenir. In this 1965 picture, No. **967** (**AWB 967B**) was crossing Fitzalan Square.

Below: The neat back-end design was exemplified by No. **987** (**AWB 987B**) at Crookes terminus in its first summer. *(Both: Author)*

Leyland Atlanteans

Above: Similar Park Royal coachwork was fitted to one Atlantean for the Department, numbered **340** (**CWB 340B**) and seen at Bridge Street. An unusual item was the opening window in the emergency door, a feature which later became standard. *(Author)*

Below: Cravens returned to bus building in 1964 through the purchase of East Lancashire Coachbuilders. The latter's distinctive designs were built at Neepsend Coachworks Ltd which was established in the city by Cravens later that year. This fine line of newly delivered Atlanteans surmounted by the depot clock featured No. **351** (**EWB 351C**) at the front. In the era of the registration year-letter it became common for batches to have their registration sequences broken, hence Nos **341/5/7/9** alongside carried the marks **CWB341/5/7/9B**. *(Richard Moore)*

Changing times

Above: The construction of the northern section of the M1 motorway created new opportunities for interurban express services, for which four 36ft Leyland Leopards with Alexander bodies were delivered in the autumn of 1968. They were the last buses to be added to the C fleet. Number **3001 (WWB 101G)** was seen at Pond Street in June 1969.

Below: Alexander coachwork was also specified for 20 Daimler Fleetlines delivered in the spring of 1972. This view of No. **259 (NWA 259K)** shows the revised fleetname style adopted under General Manager Noel MacDonald, in charge from 1969 onwards. *(Both: G H F Atkins)*

The End of an Era

Above: The 1967 Transport Act brought great changes to the bus industry, not least of which was the legalising of one-man operated double-deckers. Substantial numbers of two-door 79-seaters on extra-long Leyland and Daimler chassis were purchased, with bodies to bold new designs. This 1970 Leyland/Park Royal with the Videmat Self Service board is No. **643 (DWB 643H)**, photographed at Pond Street in 1973.

Below: There were many similar single-deckers too, and AEC Swift No. **34 (TWE 34F)** of 1968 also had Park Royal coachwork. The changes in vehicle design were as nothing compared to the end of the Sheffield Transport Department itself, absorbed into the South Yorkshire PTE on 1st April 1974. Number 34 had been repainted into the PTE's much reviled coffee and cream livery by the time of this picture in August that year, and a new era had begun.

Life After Death

Above: Many Sheffield vehicles have been preserved. None has a story as dramatic as tram No. **74**, sold to Gateshead in 1922 with the lower deck used locally as a hut after withdrawal in 1951. The 1990s restoration at the National Tramway Museum at Crich involved a full rebuild, and marrying the result with the similarly rescued top deck from car 218 and an ex-Leeds Peckham Cantilever truck.

Below: Your author was assisting at the very end of the project with the newly fabricated replacement glass advertising panels, whose frames fitted into the tops of the tudor-arch side windows. It was a memorable experience to fit the holding screws into the very same holes from which their predecessors had been removed in 1922, and history felt very tangible. The occasion served as a symbol of the quest for immortality which has ever been the lot of mankind. *(Both: John Banks)*